Hunters of the Buffalo

by

R. Stephen Irwin M.D.

Illustrations by J.B. Clemens

hancock

house

ISBN 0-88839-176-5
Copyright © 1984 R. Stephen Irwin, M.D.

Printed in Canada by: Friesen Printers

 Published simultaneously by
Hancock House Publishers Ltd.
19313 Zero Avenue, Surrey, B.C., Canada V3S 5J9
Hancock House Publishers Ltd.
1431 Harrison Ave., Blaine, Washington, U.S.A. 98230

Contents

The Series

The NATIVE HUNTER SERIES by Dr. Stephen Irwin, is taken from his major treatise

THE PROVIDERS:
Hunting and Fishing Methods of North American Natives,

from the same publisher. Many persons helped Dr. Irwin in his years of research and they are appropriately acknowledged in that major work. Similarly, an extensive bibliography is given in THE PROVIDERS.

Introduction

Until 10,000 years ago, essentially every earthling survived by hunting. By the time of Christ, 8,000 years later, only half of the human race was dependent on hunting and this number continued to dwindle until the last 300-400 years when only isolated pockets of hunting cultures existed around the world. There was a worldwide trend towards an increasing dependency on horticulture, particularly in the more temperate climates. In spite of this, of the approximately 80,000,000,000 humans who have ever lived on earth to date, 90% survived by hunting. (The word hunting here is used in the broadest sense to include fishing and trapping.) It seems inconsistent that such little is known about the technology of the economy that has been vital to the bulk of humanity. There is a lack of information on hunting, fishing and trapping techniques among hunting cultures of the last two centuries that were available for study. While the literature is replete with descriptive accounts of primitive art, social structure, mythology, linguistics, etc., apparently many early ethnographers found daily working routines essential for survival too mundane to record.

The Providers and the *Hunter Series,* is an attempt to record and to illustrate the hunting, fishing and trapping methods of the Indians and Eskimos of North America.

If some of the methods described in this book seem cruel or barbaric, we must remind ourselves that our own society is no less savage. Advanced technology may allow us to be more discreet in our slaughter, and it may be performed by proxy using select executioners, but our requirements for survival are no different from those of the native Americans. We, like they, must continue to provide.

Hunters
of the Buffalo

The American Indian: he chases buffalo on horseback, wears feathered war bonnets and beaded moccasins, lives in a tipi, and smokes a peace pipe. This cursory and inadequate description represents the stereotypic view of the Indians held by most Europeans and Americans. Even among the Plains Culture which gave rise to this archetypal Indian of movies, comics and novels, there is no typical Indian. The dour, stoic warrior with his aquiline nose and a language consisting mostly of dull-witted "hows," "ughs" and words ending in the suffix "um" is the feeble product of dramatists and romanticists. Many of the Indians' material belongings such as horses, guns and glass beads that helped to make the Western Plains Indian the so-called epitome of all that is "Indian" were actually acquired from the white man.

The Western Plains extend from the Mississippi to the base of the Rockies and from the southwest cactus country north to the conifer forests of Canada. Contained within this sizable area are several sub-ecosystems blending indistinguishably one into another. The eastern portion, with its greater rainfall, is the long-grass prairie. This blends into the short-grass prairie to the west and southwest.

The buffalo — the life-blood of the Plains Indian

This was the land of the buffalo: a huge, black inland sea of living beasts. The staggeringly huge biomass of the herds taxed the descriptive powers of early explorers. "In numbers numberless" and "like fishes in the sea" were the trite images recorded in their journals. Their individual size was awesome, their numbers vast, and their distribution wide. A mature bull might stand seven feet (2 meters) at the shoulder and weigh as much as 2,000 pounds (907 kilograms). Buffalo were gregarious animals amassing in herds of both sexes and all ages for protection. While predatory wolf packs were constantly skirting the edge of the herd to prey on young and weak animals, no enemy — except man — could challenge this herd as a whole.

The long-horned bison (*Bison antiquus*) was the first buffalo to be hunted by the Paleo hunters on the plains. Larger even than the modern American Bison (*Bison bison*), this species became extinct about 25,000 years ago for reasons that are still uncertain. The vacuum the extinction of these large ungulates produced on the Plains was filled by a gradual northward migration of the smaller American Bison from Mexico.

Buffalo were indispensable to the Plains Indians, particularly following the advent of horses, providing all necessary materials for clothing and shelter, food and a wide array of luxury items of considerable aesthetic value.

The meat of the buffalo had a beef-like quality. When prepared fresh, it was roasted, stewed, broiled, or eaten raw. Uncooked organs were particularly relished, and the task of butchering was made more enjoyable by snacking on the still-warm liver, kidneys, eyes and testicles. The chewy gristle-like hooves of unborn calves were especially savory morsels. The Blackfeet held the taste of raw liver in high esteem and felt that its palatability was further enhanced by a thin spreading of bile from the gallbladder. Though eating raw entrails was disdained by a few tribes such as the Kutenai, most Plains Indians eagerly feasted on

The buffalo.

The buffalo shared the plains and foothills with many other species of big game including elk.

the organs. The tongue was perhaps the most highly regarded piece of meat and was usually reserved for the man who had slain the animal. The marrow of the long bones was extracted and eaten with fervor, either raw or cooked. The Indians also drank the warm blood from the freshly killed animals and the clotted blood became an important ingredient in soups and puddings.

At the kill site, the frontal bone of the buffalo was bashed in with a stone maul so the brains could be scooped out and mixed with the blood that pooled in the chest cavity after butchering. This concoction was then stone-boiled by placing hot rocks in the cauldron formed by the rib cage. When the mixture congealed it was ready to eat. The stomach, filled with the mash from the herbivorous buffalo's last meal of grass, was removed, tied off at each end and roasted. When the roasted stomach was distended with heat to a football shape, it was opened and the steamy contents devoured. The kill might have taken place a long

distance from a water source, and the parched throats of thirsty hunters were relieved by cutting off the nipples of lactating udders and drinking the tepid milk.

In the spring and summer, bulls were preferred for consumption since the cows were nursing and usually quite emaciated. During the fall and winter, cows carried the choice meat and, along with yearling calves, were considered the most tender.

Although feasting on cooked fresh meat and raw organs after a kill was a satisfying and joyous occasion for the Plains Indian, of more importance to year-round survival was the meat they could preserve and store. Strips of thinly-sliced raw flesh were draped over pole frames serving the dual purpose of keeping the meat away from the hungry dogs and allowing the dry air to desiccate the flesh. The smoke from a smouldering fire under the meat rack added its preserving qualities and the result was jerky. This dehydrated meat was very light, easily transported and remarkably resistant to spoilage.

It was the culinary expertise of the Plains Indians that developed that marvelous wilderness staple, pemmican, which later became so important to white frontiersmen.

Alberta Provincial Government
A Blackfoot woman tends meat smoking on a pole frame.

Pemmican had all the qualities of transportability and pre-servability of jerky, except to a greater degree, and was of much higher nutritional quality. Pemmican was made from jerky that had been pounded with a stone maul or pemmican pounder. This finely pulverized jerky was placed in a rawhide sack, and marrow fat that had been heated to a liquid consistency was poured over the top. The hot marrow filtered down through the dried chips of meat forming a film around each piece, and acting as a preservative. Sometimes, dried berries and nuts were stirred in to add flavor, but this was thought to interfere with the preservative qualities of the mixture. The sack was then sewn shut and the seams sealed with tallow. Finally, the whole pillow-sized parcel was pounded to an even thickness of about six inches (15 centimeters) for convenient storage and easy portability.

Denver Public Library — Western History Department — Photo by Edward Curtis

An Asparoke woman scrapes a buffalo hide in front of her tipi.

Next to food, the most important commodity provided by the buffalo was the hide. Two basic tanning processes were utilized. The tough hides of bulls obtained on summer hunts were hard-tanned into what the French called *parfleche*. This stiff material was fashioned into an assortment of rigid vessels, storage containers and war shields. Even when soft-tanned, the summer bull hides were inferior to those taken in the fall and winter and would be utilized for tipi covers, ground covers, implement haftings, saddles and horse trappings, rope, bull boats, snowshoes, dance rattles and other uses where strength and durability were more important than softness and pliancy. Bull hides taken in the fall and winter were soft-tanned with the hair left on for use as blankets and robes. Most inner garments in the wardrobe of Plains Indians such as shirts, leggings, dresses and moccasins were expertly tanned from the skins of cows killed on the late fall and winter hunts. Hides tanned as soft as the finest cloths that Europe could offer were derived from young calves, and these were used for child and infant clothing as well as cradleboard coverings.

The buffalo virtually sustained life for the Plains Indians. Most items they needed were supplied by this one animal. ▶

A Mandan bull boat and paddle. These were typically made from the tough summer hides of bull buffalo.

The remainder of the buffalo carcass was ingeniously employed in the fashioning of an astonishing array of decorative and utilitarian items. Hair was braided into strong rope. The horns were cut and steamed into shape to make ladles and spoons. They also served as cups, heads for ceremonial clubs, tinder boxes and were cut into various types of ornaments. The Crow and Cheyenne possibly made bows from buffalo horns. Hooves and other cartilaginous body parts such as the muzzle, penis and sections of the rib cage were melted down to make glue. Fleshing tools were made from sharpened lower leg bones, and the scapula, when hafted to a handle, made an excellent hoe. Porous bones were used to apply paint to hides. Reinforced rib cages were used as snow sleds, and buffalo teeth were important decorative ornaments. The tendons that attached muscle to bone were dried and made into sinew for thread. Braided strands of sinew were used for bowstrings. Hollow organs such as the stomach, bladder and intestine were fashioned into all sorts of collapsible buckets, saucepans and canteens. A dried scrotum made an admirable water dipper or dance rattle. Hair combs were made from the hard dried skin of a buffalo's tongue. Even dried dung did not escape the practical and innovative eye of the Plains Indian. When burned, these buffalo chips provided a clear, hot flame with little smoke.

Hunting on Foot

Prior to the introduction of horses in the sixteenth century, Plains hunters lived what would be called a semi-nomadic existence. They had a fixed abode for the duration of the winter or longer. These shelters had a wooden frame that was covered with sticks or reeds, and was in turn covered with a layer of sod which afforded excellent year-round insulation. As was the trend among the majority of tribes throughout North America during this period, agriculture played an increasingly important role in the Indians' existence. Methods of raising corn, squash, sunflowers and beans had been learned from other tribes to the southwest who were almost totally dependent upon agriculture.

As soon as the snow melted in the spring, bands of hunters started searching for buffalo on foot. A major slaughter was not carried out, but the hunters hoped a few animals could be killed close to camp as fresh meat was direly needed at this time of year. Before embarking upon the summer hunt, a garden patch was planted. The very young, old, and the sick and infirm were left to tend the crops while the remainder of the camp went out on the hunt that would last for a month or two. In late summer the hunting party returned to their permanent encampment with a few hides and some meat. As soon as the crops were harvested and stored, the long fall hunt began. The buffalo were in their prime at this time of year, and the major kill was made to procure meat and hides for the long winter months ahead. The spoils of the hunt were returned to camp by backpacking and by dog *travois*. This limited both the distance that could be traveled and the amount that could be returned to the permanent camp. Ideally, enough meat could be dried and brought back that, along with the stores of grain, there would be ample supplies for winter. A particularly fortuitous circumstance would be a buffalo herd sharing a valley with the winter encampment. Under such circumstances, an occasional hunting foray might take place. Mostly though, the winter was a time of waiting for the spring thaw. Hopefully, it was not a period of famine.

Impounding was the preferred method of taking buffalo on the Western Plains before the advent of horses. This method was extensively used by the Assiniboine, Blackfeet, Gros Ventre, Crow and Cheyenne. A corral was constructed out of poles and situated in a coulee or clump

Stony Indian Chief from the northern plains. While he is dressed in ceremonial costume, the travois and pack horses played an important role in the band's mobility and ability to follow the moving herds of buffalo.

Dogs were commonly used as beasts of burden before horses were available.

of trees where it was not immediately evident to the shortsighted buffalo. A log ramp covered with sod to resemble the surrounding prairie floor led to the opening of the impoundment. This gradual incline dropped precipitously several feet at the lip of the corral. The drop was enough to prevent the driven beasts from running back out of the trap when they discovered their mistake. The fall was also sufficient to break the legs of the buffalo, and stumps were left standing just inside the corral to increase the

chance of death as the buffalo came pounding in — one on top of another.

Extending out onto the open prairie for a mile (1.6 kilometers) or more were two lines of stations forming a V with the apex at the mouth of the corral. These were constructed of piles of stone or buffalo chips. During an impoundment attempt, these were manned by an Indian with a robe that he might wave to induce the buffalo to stay on their fateful course toward the corral.

The stations were sparsely positioned at the outer limits of the wings: spaced infrequently enough so as not to alert the wary buffalo to the presence of a trap, but yet close enough to discourage their drifting out of the funnel. Closer to the mouth of the corral, the stations were located increasingly close together to serve as a stronger deterrent as the animals stampeded by.

Considerable time might elapse before a herd would wander close to the fatal angle between the wings, and even then success would depend on a favorable wind blowing toward the mouth of the enclosure at the time of the hunt.

Impounding was the preferred method of capturing buffalo for slaughter in many areas on the Western Plains before the advent of horses.

Intentional firings of grass carried out in the fall of the year in carefully selected areas near the mouth of the corral resulted in a new growth of grass the next year. This lusher, greener grass was an effective stimulus to get buffalo to graze in this area.

Great restraint had to be exercised in maneuvering the herd into position between the wings. Getting the great herd moving in the proper direction was a tedious undertaking done slowly and by degrees. Initially, the animals would be prodded by a lone hunter appearing on the horizon and waving a blanket; then quickly he would duck back down out of sight. On occasion, youthful runners might have to run swiftly ahead, circumnavigating the herd in an attempt to abort a turn in the wrong direction.

Even at night, after the herd was bedded down, it was nettled closer into position by dropping a folded blanket on the ground. This dull thump caused the animals to get up, edging away from this unexpected sound, and closer to the desired position. Small smouldering fires using grass or dung were lit to encourage a leisurely drift into the wings. A strain of domesticated dogs that evolved from captured coyote and wolf pups were trained to start and control buffalo stampedes into corrals, over cliffs and into other traps. Every precaution was taken not to alarm or to prematurely stampede the herd as the welfare of the entire camp during the coming winter might well depend on a successful impoundment.

As the buffalo ambled into position between the wings and headed down the funnel toward the corral, the tempo of the drive increased. The movement of the herd reached stampede proportions, egged on by yelling and blanket-waving Indians along the narrowing path, as the edge of the impoundment was neared. By the time the lead buffalo had sensed the trap, it was already too late. In spite of sharp braking efforts, it was carried over the brink by the sheer momentum of the herd behind. Panic and confusion now blocked the buffalo's normal instincts, and this further hastened their demise. The air was so choked with dust, and the animals so tightly packed between the collapsing arms of the V, that the herd would now charge blindly into the corral.

The impoundment had to be stoutly built. The usual determining factor for the size of a corral was the number of families in the camp. Occasionally, the more moderately-sized corrals were filled to such a capacity that some of the last buffalo to enter could escape by merely clambering over the backs of their companions and on over the sides of the corral.

Once securely in the impoundment, all of the participants of the hunt triumphantly descended on the corral to perch on its edge and start killing the buffalo with bows and arrows and lances. An attempt to make the annihilation complete was made because it was feared that any escapee would warn other buffalo of the trap, and so render it useless in the future.

An added inducement for the buffalo to head in the proper direction toward the corral was achieved with a decoy by some tribes. Two Indian hunters draped hides over their bodies: one of a buffalo calf and the other of a wolf. A simulated attack on the buffalo calf by the wolf was then staged. This pantomine dramatized with bellowing, duped the buffalo into coming to the aid of the distressed calf. Such productions often were successful in coaxing the herd in the correct direction. It was essential that these human decoys were also quite fleet of foot to escape the animals' charge. In case one of the decoys was forced into the corral by the stampeding herd, a small portal was constructed for a hasty exit.

A variation of the impoundment method of slaughtering buffalo is what the Blackfeet called a "*piskin*." Literally translated, this means "deep blood kettle" and it utilized natural features of the terrain. Instead of being stampeded into a corral, the buffalo were driven over the edge of a tall cliff where they would fall to their death, or at least be so maimed that they could be easily subdued. Suitable cliffs were carefully selected and tactics for getting the herd started in the direction of the cliff, and stampeded over the edge, were essentially the same as used in the impoundment method. The women waited below the cliff out of the way of the tumbling buffalo ready with their skinning knives and *travois* for transporting the butchered carcasses back to the camp. As soon as the last buffalo plunged to his death, the women quickly moved in to club the survivors and go efficiently about their task of skinning and butchering. A few days after the drive, the stench of decaying blood and offal carried for some distance downwind. A host of scavengers ranging from eagles to coyotes to the lowly carrion beetle, moved in to clean up the remains. Only after a thorough purging by sun, wind and rain would nature, together with time restore the site for another use. The Blackfeet continued using their *piskin* long after horses were available primarily because of the older tribe members' reluctance to let tradition die. The locations of several of these buffalo jumps in the western United States are known, and the Madison Site near Butte, Montana is now a state memorial.

The foot-surround could be attempted on a windless day, and while it did not involve a wholesale slaughter as the drives did, it was an effective means of killing a few buffalo. Everyone in the camp completely encircled a small group of cows and calves to separate them from the main herd. The ring of hunters gradually closed in on the small herd, and with luck could get within thirty or forty yards (27 or 37 meters) of the nearsighted animals. When the buffalo became aware of the hunters, the animals instinctively would start milling about searching for internal protection among the herd. Capitalizing on this confusion, the Indians were afforded some easy bow and arrow shots. Eventually, the flustered herd would break through the lines and escape, but not without leaving several of their numbers behind dead or wounded.

The Ojibwa, Winnebago, Iowa and Santee Sioux of the eastern long-grass prairie effectively utilized the fire-surround. A band of hunters ignited the dry prairie grass around a herd of buffalo. The result was a ring of fire with select segments of the circle not burning. As the buffalo fled the enclosing fire through these "safe" avenues of escape, they were forced to literally run a gauntlet of armed hunters who had been stationed there to shoot the beasts as they fled.

Stalking was usually accomplished by a hunter down on all fours with a wolf skin draped over his body. This allowed an approach to within bow range of a portion of the herd. Wolves constantly prowled the fringes of buffalo herds, and while they posed a threat to an individual calf or a sick or injured adult lagging behind the main herd, healthy, mature animals scarcely paid attention to their presence. This provided just the cover the wolf skin-draped stalker needed for his approach.

Buffalo are almost constantly on the move, their wanderings necessitated by the rapidity with which they deplete the grass supply. Ambush tactics were usually foiled by the fact that these herd wanderings were totally random and completely unpredictable. Still, even on the open plains, there existed certain draws or passes that were frequently traversed by the herds. These represented nothing more than the easiest way of passing from one point to another, or perhaps they led to a scarce watering hole. The pounding of countless hooves on the ground in such places resulted in deeply worn ruts. In these furrows, a hunter smeared with mud or dust for camouflage could get a close shot at a passing buffalo by exercising patience and lying in wait.

Primitive hunters were adept at using natural barriers

or inclement conditions to hinder the mobility of a pursued animal. The Plains Indians were no exception. Expert swimmers were able to kill buffalo using a knife when they overtook them swimming wide expanses of water such as the Missouri River. The occasional winter hunting foray usually resulted when a herd was discovered wintering in a valley with deep snow. The buffalo were ungainly under such conditions and were readily subdued by snowshoe-clad hunters. Nor were sharp buffalo hooves ideally designed to gain a purchase on the slippery ice of lakes or rivers. Tribes along the Missouri, Platte, Arkansas and Kansas Rivers made a practice of herding buffalo onto the frozen rivers, surrounding them and killing the handicapped beasts. The translation of the Plains Cree term for this type of hunting was "wolf pound." Undoubtedly, the inspiration, among the Plains Cree at least, for this method of hunting was from observing packs of wolves practice the same techniques.

Hunting on Horseback

By the time of the first Anglo-American exploration of the continent west of the Mississippi by Lewis and Clark in 1805, horses were in general use among most tribes of the Western Plains. Not only did the Plains Indians possess horses, but the Lewis and Clark expedition described a sophisticated horse culture replete with trappings, methods of training, experience in breeding (the Nez Perce developed the Appaloosa strain), many legends and unparalleled expertise in riding.

The travois, used to carry buffalo meat or other supplies — even babies.

The horses that roamed the North American Continent during the Pleistocene Era had become extinct. The Plains Indians first saw horses in 1541, when Francisco Coronado, searching for the fabled Seven Cities of Cibola and their reputed vast treasures of gold, pushed north into Kansas from the Rio Grande Valley. That same year, the mounted De Soto Expedition reached the Trinity River in Texas. These Spanish Conquistadores with their horses were greeted by the Indians with fascination and no small degree of fear. They held the horses in particular awe and called them "big dogs", "elk dogs" or "mystery dogs." It was probably not, however, the horses of these early Spanish expeditions that were the ancestors of the later Plains Indian horses. The Spanish did not use mares in military excursions such as these, and hence there was no brood stock to establish a herd. Rather, the first Indian horses were probably derived from Spanish cattle ranches established along the Rio Grande River in the seventeenth century. Indians of the area were employed as cowboys and not infrequently made off with some horses, which they drove north and traded to free-ranging tribes. Also, the

Oshkosh Public Museum — Photo by Roland Reed

A group of Blackfeet move camp in search of more buffalo in Cut Bank County, Montana.

Pueblo Indians revolted against the Spanish occupation of their territory in 1680 and drove all the Spaniards out of that frontier province for twelve years. During the uprising, large herds of horses were taken by Indians and were rapidly dispersed northward through thefts and trades.

The semi-nomadic Plains tribes who had depended partly on agriculture and partly on the buffalo for subsistence were quick to realize the advantages horses offered in hunting buffalo. They soon learned that horses could outrun a buffalo in the open. It became relatively easy to cut off a few buffalo from the main herd and to kill them from horseback. The procurement of meat became not only easier but possible in any season. In unusually lean times when no meat was available, a nag pack horse might even be slaughtered to ward off starvation. The entire camp mounted on horses could now follow the meanderings of the large herds. More fresh meat could be obtained and larger stores of dried meat could be transported. The means of this new mobility, the horse, ironically became one of the very reasons for it. The grass supply for a radius of several miles about the encampment was rapidly depleted by the horses, and thus necessitated a move to new pastures.

The tipi became the ideal shelter for these increasingly nomadic people and soon totally replaced the sod covered hogans. Even the size of the tipis was affected by the use of horses. Many parts of the Plains were treeless, and tipi poles had to be carried from one campsite to the next. It was these tipi poles that formed the legs of the travois and, when only dogs were available to pull these, the tipi poles were of necessity quite short. With horse travois, longer poles could be used; the horses could pull larger and heavier hide tipi covers, and living space was proportionately expanded. Stones weighted the bases of the erected tipis to the ground, and of course these "tipi rings" of stone were left behind when camp was moved. Even today, the age of a campsite can be distinguished as dating from the pre or post-horse era by the diameter of the rings of stone.

Milwaukee Public Museum
A group of Blackfeet return to camp after a buffalo hunt — near Cut Bank, Montana.

In an amazingly short period of time, the Plains Indians underwent a metamorphosis from somewhat beggarly foot hunters to one of the premier equestrian peoples in the history of the world. Their free and adventurous lifestyle has continued to capture the imaginations and envy of more sedentary people everywhere. The primarily agricultural people in the fringe areas abandoned their lifestyles to take up the nomadic life of the buffalo culture. The Sioux forsook their rich rice-producing area of the Minnesota Lake country and moved into the Dakotas. A separate

33

A good buffalo horse had to be not only fast and strong but also brave enough to barge into a thundering herd, and yet intelligent enough to shy away from a wounded buffalo intent on goring.

group, the Eastern Sioux, remained behind. The Piegan, Blood and Blackfeet moved south out of Alberta, Canada into Montana. The Comanches came out of the Colorado Canyonlands onto the Southern Plains and took to horseback as full-time bison hunters. Coeur d'Alene, Nez Perce and Salish made excursions onto the high plains to supplement their salmon diet, as did the Yakima, Walla Walla and Cayuse. Though the Pawnee, Arikara and Mandan continued to grow corn, they too visited the buffalo country to hunt, whereas prior to owning horses they mostly traded for meat and hides. A universal sign language was invented to breach the communication barrier. As a result, this land of the buffalo — the Western Plains — became a melting pot of diverse Indian cultures.

A good buffalo horse had to be not only fast and strong but brave enough to barge into a thundering herd, and intelligent enough to shy away from a wounded buffalo intent on goring. An animal like this was the most highly prized possession any Plains Indian could own. The presence of such a horse within a camp could easily spell the difference between an easy life and famine. As warfare, raiding and horse-stealing became the norm among Plain tribes, constant vigilance was required in guarding a top buffalo horse.

Riding was essentially bareback with just a buffalo hide-pad strapped on the horse's back. The leather belly cinch was left loose enough that the rider could wrap his legs underneath for stability and leave his hands free to manage a weapon. Pressure with the knees and shifting of the rider's weight guided the horse. A rope of braided hair was tied to the horse's lower jaw and tucked into the rider's waistband. The halter rope was quite long, twenty-five or thirty feet (8 or 9 meters), and if the rider was thrown off he was afforded the chance of regaining his mount by catching this long rope as it trailed by.

The most common weapon used against buffalo from

horseback was the short bow. The Pawnees had a legend saying they received the bow from the moon and the sun gave them arrows. The true origin of the bow and arrow on the Western Plains is uncertain, but there is no doubt that it developed into one of the world's finest hunting instruments. Typically, Plains bows had double or recurved tips which gave a decided improvement to the cast. This shortened the working limbs to make the bow easier to use from horseback, and at the same time acted as a lever to aid in drawing. Osage orange (a member of the mulberry family) and Oregan yew were the preferred bow woods of most Plains tribes. The brushy osage orange tree, in particular, grew in river bottoms throughout most of the Western Plains. Still, in some areas, select bow wood was scarce, and smart Indian hunters were perpetually on the lookout for good pieces. They usually owned a supply of bow staves in varying phases of preparation. The raw materials, as well as finished bows, were common trade items among Plains tribes. The osage orange was difficult to work because of twists in the grain and, indeed, it may have been this characteristic that dictated that Plains bows be short. Nonetheless, the short bow, seldom exceeding 2½ feet (.8 meters) in length, proved to be the ideal weapon for the Plains hunter. And osage orange, in spite of its brushy and gnarled appearance, had superior properties of elasticity and tensile strength that far exceeded its shortcomings. Considerably more power was derived from these bows by gluing green sinew strips to the backs. As the strips dried and created tension along the arc of the bow, power was greatly increased. Elk antlers, mountain sheep horns and possibly buffalo horns were also used to make bows — at least among the Shoshonis, Blackfeet, Crow and Nez Perce. It is doubtful that they offered as much in performance as they did in prestige. Certainly they were more difficult to make than wood bows. Sinew from the buffalo's loin was the favorite material for bow strings.

Serviceberry, gooseberry, cherry, and wild currant were the materials most commonly used for arrow shafts. These were cut in the late winter when the sap was running so the sticks would not split while drying. Where available, cane and certain durable reeds were also used. Fletching was obtained from the feathers of some great bird of prey such as a hawk or eagle, and it was hoped that the hunting prowess of these predators would be transferred to the arrows. Material for arrow tips varied from area to area; but bone and the tips of antler tines were used as well as several stone types including flint, chert, jasper and obsidian.

Archery practice was introduced early into child rearing. One of the first toys a young boy would be given was a tiny, but functional, bow and set of arrows. All sorts of bow and arrow games were devised. In one, a youngster shot an arrow into the ground some distance away. His companions would then shoot at this arrow and the one coming the closest was declared the winner, and this would start the next round. Most Plains youth were accomplished bow shots by early adolescence.

On the other hand, some Southern Plains tribes used lances from horseback on buffalo hunts. The practicality of this custom undoubtedly arose from a paucity of good bow wood amidst plentiful cane for lances. Unlike spears, lances were made for thrusting instead of throwing, and were not released from the grip.

Buffalo were not migratory in a seasonal manner. They were better classified as unpredictable wanderers. As astute as Plains Indians were in observing animal movements, there is no record of their having detected an established migratory pattern. Such frequent moves from one camp to another were required in the nomadic pursuit of buffalo that the tipi poles used to form the travois were worn down on their butt ends so much they had to be replaced two or three times in some years.

The Plains buffalo hunters' thorough knowledge of the

buffalo's anatomy enhanced their expertise. Broad ribs that nearly overlapped each other in the expiratory phase of respiration presented an almost impenetratable barrier to the thoracic cavity and its vital organs. A more feasible approach to the heart-lung area was behind the rib cage with the line of aim directed forward. This avenue pierced soft structures such as intestine and diaphragm on the way to the heart, lungs and great vessels.

Just as with the various drive and surround methods, considerable team effort was required for a hunt. Various organizational rules were necessary, and individual hunting efforts had to be suspended to insure a successful camp hunt. A policing unit of young braves known as dog soldiers was formed to effect these rules. The usual superstitions and ritualistic preparation that preceded most Indian hunting forays were particularly paramount to the buffalo hunt.

Scouts were forever searching for buffalo. Once a herd was located, the terrain was studied for the best approach and for the probable escape routes the buffalo would attempt. The scout then rode jubilantly into camp and announced his discovery. Older braves, familiar with the intricacies of the terrain, drew up a plan for the hunt, and, after meeting certain spiritual obligations, the men left for the chase. In a camp with many horses, the slower animals were ridden to the hunt. The fastest mounts were led so they would be fresh for the sprint into the herd.

An upwind approach to within a quarter of a mile (.4 kilometers) or closer was made. Coulees or buttes were used for concealment to get as close as possible to the grazing buffalo before the final dash. As soon as the buffalo herd sensed danger and stampeded, the horses were whipped into a gallop and could usually overtake the fleeing beasts within a half of a mile (.8 kilometers). On occasion, an approach from two directions was used to confuse the herd and to delay their attempted escape, or perhaps to cause part of the herd to run toward their pursuers.

Once the hunters caught up with the herd, the horses were urged into the fast-moving melee of dust, flying hooves and bawling beasts. Several buffalo were separated from the main body and surrounded. It was easier to control the speed and direction of this smaller group.

The buffalo horse sidled up to the flank of a buffalo and offered its rider a shot with the bow or a thrust with the lance into the posterior rib area. All the while, the horse anticipated the goring attempt that was certain to occur as soon as the buffalo perceived that it had been wounded. Sometimes, repeated arrow-shooting or lance thrusts into vital areas were required to subdue an animal. Even a small cow could be an imposing animal to kill. Mortally wounded buffalo displayed a remarkable tenacity for life, and defied the gravity of their injuries. As soon as the hunter was convinced that the buffalo had been injured to the point that it could no longer keep up with the stampede, he would spur his horse on to another quarry.

The entire chase was fraught with danger for both horse and rider. The ubiquitous prairie dog holes posed the threat of tripping the galloping horse and throwing the hunter to the ground to be pulverized by churning hooves. The only thing to do in such a situation was to grab two handfuls of belly fur on a buffalo passing overhead and hang on until dragged clear of the thundering fracas.

Young calves in the herd frequently could not keep up with the fleet-footed adults and would tire quickly. Exhausted, they would hide in the tall prairie grass. Young boys, not yet old enough for the main hunt, would follow along and sharpen their hunting skills on these hapless, trembling animals.

The chase would end quickly: either when enough buffalo had been dropped or, more frequently, when the mount was so winded that urging it on was likely to result in its stumbling from exhaustion. The mounts were checked and slowly walked back across the massacre site. Their nostrils would flare and their sides heave in an attempt to regain their wind. Slathers of sweaty foam would drip from their necks and flanks. Buffalo carcasses lay strewn across the prairie. Though feathered with arrows and mortally wounded, many buffalo still had a breath of life remaining. They would arch their backs and bristle when the hunters approached, and then fall to the ground from loss of blood. These bleary-eyed beasts were finished off by the less successful participants of the hunt. Not infrequently, there were also moans from braves with broken limbs, concussions and other injuries. Horses too, were often killed in the chase.

Young boys would come along after the main hunt and sharpen their hunting skills on young calves hiding in the prairie grass.

The hunters, euphoric from the excitement of the chase, tallied their kills, swapped tales and boasted of their bravery. The women, who had been hiding downwind, came forth to start their task of skinning and butchering. Excitedly, they would scurry about among the fallen carcasses looking for those containing their husbands' arrows. From these, they would be entitled to the choice parts, but were expected to share the remainder with widows, the elderly and with the families of less fortunate hunters.

The cuts of meat from butchered buffalo were wrapped in the green hides, and this bundle was lashed onto a *travois* for transport to camp. If camp was some distance away, and if the hunt was quite successful, the tipis might be taken down and moved to the kill site. If this was the case, or if so many animals had been slain that not all of the meat and hides could be brought into camp before nightfall, a sentinel was posted with each remaining carcass. Women and children tended small fires, and when wolves, coyotes or other predators lurked too close to the slain buffalo, they would toss a tuft of dried grass on the fire to cause a short burst of flame. This was usually sufficient to drive away hungry prowlers — at least for a while. As the scene of activity shifted back to camp, the scant remains of buffalo left by the Indians were claimed by scavengers. The carnivores just below man on the food chain, the wolves, foxes and coyotes, were the first to feast on the remains. Their quarrels and fights were heard through the night. At first light, the diurnal members of the clean-up crew, such as eagles and ravens, completed the task. There was no waste of nature's bounty.

Meanwhile in the Indian camp, night overtook the operation as the last loads were dumped on the growing mounds of fresh meat beside each tipi. An orange glow from many fires encompassed the camp. Choice cuts of meat were roasted over open fires. Dogs, tied up so they couldn't raid the meat piles, were tossed some less-than-prime cuts to quiet their howling. Children, their faces smeared with grease, sucked the congealed marrow out of long bones that had been roasted over hot embers. Men laughed, sang, danced and bragged while waiting for a calf's head to bake buried in the ground under a pile of hot coals. It had been a good day this time, and it was a time of merriment. There was plenty to eat. The buffalo hunt had been a success.

It is probably true that no single animal ever exerted a

stronger influence on human culture than did the buffalo on the Indians of the Western Plains. Buffalo numbers were greatly decimated after the white man came to the Plains. The introduction of firearms was not so much the culprit as was the desire for hides. Buffalo-hide overcoats were both practical and fashionable, and many thousands of the durable hides were tanned and made into machine belting for the mills of industrial New England and Europe. The hide trade resulted in rampant killing and waste by whites and Indians alike. Hide-stripped carcasses were left to rot, and Indians depended on trade staples as the mainstay of their diet and to fulfill most of their needs. Certainly, white traders encouraged these actions. Yet, in retrospect, it seems likely that the ultimate fate of the buffalo was sealed when horses were first obtained by Plains Indians. Agricultural practices, becoming more prevalent and increasingly complex and productive, were suddenly abandoned for an easier and more glamorous lifestyle. A highly efficient harvesting method was pitted against a resource that was renewable, but which nonetheless, started showing signs of giving out before the final years of slaughter began. Enormous quantities of buffalo were killed by mounted hunters to feed a rapidly increasing Plains population who were almost totally dependent on this single animal for their existence. Increased affluence also led to increased waste. With this situation, the die was cast. The hide trade served only to hasten the buffalo's inevitable demise.

Hunting other Game

The significance of all other game hunted by Plains Indians pales when compared to the buffalo. Antelope were probably next in importance. Certainly, they were next in abundance, and indeed probably even exceeded buffalo in total numbers. Being a small animal of less contrasting coloration, and banding in small groups instead of vast herds, they received less attention from the early chroniclers than did the buffalo, and they could not be overtaken by horse-mounted hunters. A mature buck would not exceed seventy or eighty pounds (32 or 36 kilograms) and did not provide much meat for the effort expended in slaughtering one. Furthermore, their hide tanned poorly and made inferior leather.

Since antelope were not adaptable to horseback hunting, the brush corral method of harvesting persisted well into the post contact era. A herd of animals was

The antelope's curiosity was used against it in this commonly employed method of hunting.

Pronghorn antelope, mountain goat and big horn sheep also shared the plains and foothills and were hunted.

Sharptail grouse

Canada geese

Wolf

Sage grouse

stampeded into flimsy corrals made of piled-up sagebrush with a funnel at the entrance, not dissimilar in configuration to those used for buffalo. Such agile animals could have easily vaulted these enclosures, but some quirk of their nature prevented them from doing so.

The antelope's innate curiosity made them easy prey for a hunter hiding just below the skyline of a ridge, waving some eagle feathers on a stick so they could be seen by a herd in the valley below. Their insatiable curiosity, piqued by this unfamiliar object waving in the breeze, prompted them to walk to within easy ambush range. White plainsmen were taught this method of hunting by the Indians and called it "tolling for antelope."

Rocky mountain bighorn sheep have not always been the timid dwellers of high and remote places they are today. Prior to the encroachment of white civilization, they frequented bluffs along the Yellowstone and Little Missouri Rivers and inhabited the Black Hills as recently as 1860. They were not only plentiful, but probably the easiest of all hooved game to stalk and kill with a bow and arrow. The Shoshoni were adept at luring sheep into close bow range during the rut by clashing stones together to simulate the sound of rams battering their horns during a supremacy fight.

The Cheyenne, Blackfeet and Arapahoes all set nooses in timbered areas to catch elk in a manner identical to the method used by Athapaskan tribes in Canada for caribou.

The grizzly bear elicited well deserved respect from Plains Indians and was seldom hunted before firearms were available.

Rabbits and prairie dogs made challenging targets for aspiring young buffalo hunters. A more effective method for waylaying prairie dogs was to plug their burrow exits with manure or grass and then dig a basin around the hole. This basin was filled with water, and when the plug was removed a torrent of water rushed into the hole. This rapidly evicted the soaked occupants, who were clubbed by a waiting hunter as they emerged.

The Western Plains were rife with prairie chickens. The famous chronicler of western Indian life, George Catlin, described in his journals (1832-1839) how grass fires were used to harvest these fowl. The prairie chickens, capable of only short, sporadic flights, kept flying ahead of the advancing fire and landing until the flames again caught up with them. When a draw containing some trees was encountered, the birds would alight in the branches hoping, at this height, to gain a longer reprieve from the fire. Hunters, armed with bows and arrows, capitalized on this by hiding in camouflage among the trees and shooting the prairie chickens as they arrived. Catlin did not state if the fires were from natural causes or if they were intentionally set.

Part of the Western Plains is within the central flyway, and is visited seasonally by tens of thousands of migrating ducks and geese. As they made brief rest stops on the prairie potholes during their flight, they were too tempting for Plains Indian hunters to ignore. It was while noting how

Sinew-wrapped bundles of rushes were made to closely resemble canvasback ducks and used as decoys.

Birds of prey were captured by hunters lying in wait in a concealed pit that was baited.

these wary waterfowl trustingly splashed down among their own kind on a lake that the idea of a duck decoy was born. Excavations of Lovelock Cave in Nevada's Humboldt Range in 1924 yielded almost a dozen decoys made of bulrushes: woven, shaped and tied to realistically resemble canvasback ducks. Long white feathers were inserted along the sides to copy the male's flanks, and black and rust pigments were used to color the head and back. These decoys were set at the edge of reeds in open water while the hunter hid in vegetation closer to shore. His black hair sprinkled with cattail pollen to blend better with his surroundings, the Indian hunter would dabble his fingers in the water to mimic the sound of feeding waterfowl.

Among common items of barter, only horses exceeded eagle feathers in trade value. Feathers were used for personal adornment and were symbolic of wealth and accomplishment for the owner. Eagles and hawks were caught by hand. A pit large enough to conceal a hunter was dug. While the hunter crouched in the pit, his companion covered the top with a lattice-work of brush, and baited the trap with a dead rabbit. The concealed hunter had only to wait until some bird of prey was attracted to the bait. He then sprang through the brush covering and grabbed the unsuspecting bird by the legs.

The buffalo culture was doomed by the introduction of horses. The culture flickered for a brief two-hundred years. Like the sea-faring Vikings and the knights of King Arthur, the Plains Indians life style has excited the imaginations of men ever since. What would the Lewis and Clark Expedition have found if horses had never been re-introduced into the New World? There would have probably existed a culture of sedentary people practicing agriculture and exhibiting decreasing dependency on hunting as a way of providing. History would have been robbed of one of its most colorful chapters.

Index